Mayer's Best of Vermont

Photography, concept, text and design © 1997 by Alois Mayer
All Rights Reserved
Published by Mayer Photographics, Inc.
HCR 34 Box 2357
Rutland, Vermont 05701
Printed in Italy
ISBN 0-9657583-0-3

- Silk Road Covered Bridge.
- The First Congregational Church, built in 1806.
- Site of the historic Catamount Tavern, 1767.
- Monument Avenue; this graceful fence lines one of Vermont's most renowned burial grounds.

Historic Old Bennington

3

Historic Bennington

- The 306 ft. Bennington Battle Monument & Seth Warner Statue as seen from Monument Avenue.
- The Bennington Museum, Grandma Moses Schoolhouse Museum & the American Spirit Statue.

Manchester and Arlington

- The Historic Equinox Hotel, Manchester.
- Covered Bridge near former home of artist Norman Rockwell, West Arlington.
- Chiselville Covered Bridge in Sunderland.
- Manchester Village in Autumn.

- Robert Todd Lincoln's Hildene, Manchester; Abraham Lincoln's descendants lived here.
- Cross Country Skiing at Hildene.
- Alpine Slide, Bromley Mountain.
- Stratton Mountain Resort.

Manchester and the Mountains

Maple Sugaring

In late winter, when warm days are followed by cold nights, the sap of the sugar maple begins to flow. Farmers tap the maple trees and hang buckets to collect the sap. The gathered sap is then transported in large tanks with a team of horses, or more often with tractors, for boiling in the sugarhouse. A more modern method is the use of plastic tubing to run the sap to the sugar shack. It takes about 30-40 gallons of the watery maple sap to make a single gallon of the famous Vermont Maple Syrup.

Brattleboro: a team of horses at the Thurber Farm.
Mendon: Sugarbush with snow covered buckets.
Hartland: boiling sap at the Richardson Farm.

- Vivid autumn foliage, West Dover.
- Wilmington, Main Street Bridge decorated with flowers.
- Aerial scene of Whitingham Lake in view of Haystack Mtn. & Mount Snow.
- Aerial view of Mount Snow-Haystack Ski Resort, Deerfield Valley, West Dover.

West Dover, Wilmington
&
Mount Snow - Haystack

Brattleboro & Guilford

Hogback, Marlboro Williamsville Newfane & Grafton

- Side view of the Creamery Bridge, built in 1878, it crosses the Whetstone Brook in Brattleboro.
- Green River Falls, Green River, Guilford.
- Brattleboro in view of the Connecticut River.
- Williamsville Covered Bridge, built around 1870, crosses the Rock River in Williamsville.
- Hogback Mountain, Marlboro, site of the renown 100 mile view.
- Windham County Courthouse, built in 1825, located on the Village Green in Newfane.
- The Old Tavern, village of Grafton.

Brockways
Mills

Rockingham

Springfield

Windsor

- Green Mountain Flyer Scenic Railroad at Brockways Mills Gorge, Rockingham.
- Bartonsville Covered Bridge, built in 1870, spans the Williams River, Rockingham.
- Springfield; this beautiful Methodist stone church is located in the center of town.
- The historic Old Constitution House in Windsor. This is the Birthplace of Vermont.
- The Windsor - Cornish Covered Bridge spans the Connecticut River.

Village of Weston

This lovely village is nestled in the hills of the upper West River Valley and is listed in the National Register of Historic Places.

Weston is home of the renowned Vermont Country Store and numerous unique country-shops, craft shops and museums. The Weston Playhouse is one of the state's oldest summer theaters.

- Aerial view of Weston.
- The Weston Playhouse.
- The Vermont Country Store.
- The West River, Mill Pond Falls.
- The Weston Village Store.

Ludlow, Okemo & Plymouth

- Scenic view of Okemo Mountain Ski Resort.
- Baptist Church on the Village Green, Ludlow.
- Swimming holes at Buttermilk Falls, Ludlow.

- Plymouth Notch, State Historic Site, Birthplace of Calvin Coolidge, 30th. President of the U.S.
- Echo Lake, Route 100 in Tyson, Plymouth.

Quechee

- Quechee Gorge, Quechec.
- Balloon Festival, Quechee.
- Village of Norwich.

Woodstock & Pomfret

- Billings Farm and Museum, Woodstock.
- Farmstead in Autumn, W. Woodstock.
- The Sleepy Hollow Farm in Pomfret.
- Quaint Town Office, Village of Pomfret.

Woodstock

- Woodstock Inn and Resort, on The Green.
- Congregational Church, Elm Street.
- Norman Williams Library and Windsor County Courthouse, on The Green.

- One of Woodstock's many beautiful homes.
- Middle Bridge spans the Ottauquechee River.
- Richmond House on Elm Street.

Reading, Woodstock & Killington

- Holstein cows at the Jenne Farm in Reading.
- Winter's magic, Middle Bridge, Woodstock.
- A serene landscape. Jenne Farm, Reading.

- Killington's "Outer Limits," the famous double diamond trail on Bear Mountain.
- Killington Skyeship, a high-speed heated eight passenger gondola.
- Aerial view of Killington, depicting 4 peaks of the 7- Mountain Complex.

Killington - Rutland Region

- Scenic wayside, Cream Hill Road, Mendon.
- Baker- or Thundering Brook Falls, Killington.
- Pico Peak reflects in Kent Pond, Killington.

- Scenic view of Rutland City and Blue Ridge Mountain.
- Saint Bridget's Church in view of Pico, West Rutland.
- Pico Peak, Killington & Mendon Mountain, prominent members of the Green Mountain Range.

Bomoseen, Proctor, Hubbardton & Orwell

- Sailing regatta, Lake Bomoseen.
- Wilson's Castle, Proctor.
- Vermont Marble Exhibit, Proctor.

- Hubbardton Battle Monument & Visitor Center.
- Revolutionary War Enactment, Orwell.
- Mount Independence Visitor Center in Orwell.

State Historic Sites

Brandon & Dunmore

- County sporting goods store, Route 30, Whiting.
- View from the Village Green in Brandon.
- Aerial view of Lake Dunmore, depicting Branbury State Park and the Waterhouse's Marina.

Middlebury Salisbury & Weybridge

- The Shard Villa, Salisbury.
- Otter Creek Falls, Marble Works, Middlebury.
- Morgan Horse Farm in Weybridge.
- Pulp Mill Covered Bridge, built 1808-1820, Weybridge-Middlebury.
- The Sugarbush Express, scenic excursion train at the Middlebury Train Station.

Middlebury
Ripton

- Scenic view of Middlebury College, Middlebury.
- Le Chateau, Middlebury College, Middlebury.
- The Robert Frost Cabin, Ripton.
- Bread Loaf Inn, Middlebury College Bread Loaf Campus in Ripton.

The Champlain Valley; Chimney Point...

to Charlotte

- Champlain Bridge, Crown Point - Chimney Point, Addison.
- Otter Creek Falls, Macdonough Shipyard, Vergennes.
- Town Farm Bay in view of the Adirondack Mountains.
- McNeil Cove, Charlotte, Vt. - Essex N.Y. Ferry, Charlotte.

Killington, Rochester & Granville

- Rochester, view of Killington and Pico from North Hollow.
- Cow crossing, Route 100, in Lower Granville.
- Picturesque wayside, flowers & split rail fence.
- Moss Glen Falls, Green Mountain National Forest, Granville.

Warren, Waitsfield and

Sugarbush

- Warren Bridge, spans the Mad River, Warren.
- Haying at the Lareau Farm in Waitsfield.
- Country road in autumn, East Warren.
- Aerial view of Sugarbush Ski Resort, depicting Sugarbush South Basin and Sugarbush North.
- Mount Ellen's renowned upper FIS double diamond expert ski trail.
- Waitsfield Village in view of Sugarbush North.
- Sleigh riding at the Lareau Farm in Waitsfield.

Barre, Granite Center of the World

Granite carved by American and European craftsmen.
- Robert Burns Memorial, panels reflect Burns' Poetry.
- Statue honoring Italian-Americans who have enriched this city, region and state.
- Youth Victorious Statue, located in the Barre City Park.
- Rock of Ages, the world's largest granite quarries.

Montpelier, Capital of Vermont

- Scenic view of Montpelier.
- The Pavilion, Vt. Historical Society Museum.
- Vermont State House.
- Beautiful autumn display at the Morse Farm.

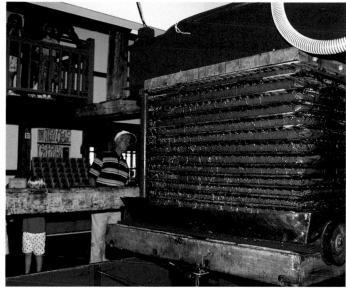

- Waterbury Ctr., in view of 4,083 ft. Camel's Hump.
- Cider Press at the Cold Hollow Cider Mill in Waterbury Center.
- October snow. Red maple in autumn splendor.
- Autumn in Pleasant Valley. View of 4,393 ft. Mt. Mansfield, Vermont's highest mountain.

Waterbury Center, Camel's Hump & Mount Mansfield

Village of Stowe & Mount Mansfield

Stowe is one of New England's most renowned resort villages.

- Autumn spectacle. The season's first snow on Mount Mansfield.
- Aerial view of Stowe village.
- Beautiful Bingham Falls, Stowe.
- Emily's Covered Bridge spans the Gold Brook at Stowe Hollow.

Village of Stowe
&
Mt. Mansfield

- The exquisite spire of the Stowe Community Church in view of Mount Mansfield.
- The Stowe Gondola ascends Mt. Mansfield amid vivid autumn foliage.
- Aerial view of the village and Mt. Mansfield in winter.
- Surveying the view. Mount Mansfield, elevation of 4,393 feet, is Vermont's highest mountain.
- Stowe Alpine Slide on Little Spruce Mtn.
- Stowe Recreation Path in view of Mount Mansfield.

Trapp Family Lodge, Stowe

A Mountain Resort in the European Tradition. By the family that inspired "The Sound of Music."

Smugglers' Notch & Mt. Mansfield

- Smugglers' Notch, Vermont's historic and most scenic mountain pass, Stowe.
- Moonlight in Vermont, Mt. Mansfield, Pleasant Valley.
- Aerial view of Smugglers' Notch Ski Resort also depicts the notch between Madonna Mtn. and Mount Mansfield.

Burlington &
Lake Champlain

- View of the Old Mill, University Place, Burlington.
- Statue in honor of Chief Gray Lock, Battery Park.
- Battery Park, view of Juniper Island & Lake Champlain.
- Lake Champlain Balloon Festival, Essex Junction.
- Ira Allen Chapel, University Place, Burlington.
- Scenic Line Ferry, Burlington Vermont - Port Kent N.Y.

Burlington & Lake Champlain

- Burlington Boathouse and the Spirit of Ethan Allen II cruise boat, viewed here from the beautiful Waterfront Park.
- Church Street Market Place.
- Gardens at the Boathouse entrance.

The Queen City

- Downtown Burlington in view of Shelburne Bay.
- Lake Champlain & Burlington in view of Mt. Mansfield.

Grand Isle

- Lake Champlain sunset. This beautiful lake is 107 miles long.
- S. Hero & Lake Champlain in view of the Adirondack Mountains.
- Statue of French explorer Samuel de Champlain, Isle La Motte.
- North Hero in view of Alburg & Swanton. The Gut lies between
  S. & N. Hero and connects the open lake with the Inland Sea.

St. Albans
Montgomery
Jay Peak

- Saint Albans Bay in view of Saint Albans.
- Bronze Fountain, Taylor Park, Saint Albans.
- Fuller Covered Bridge (1890), Montgomery.
- Aerial Tramway, approaches the lofty summit, Jay Peak.

- Bull Moose in early morning, Shrewsbury.
- Whitetail Deer in late afternoon, Enosburg.
- Red Fox, Pico, Killington.
- Elks, Derby.

Wildlife

Cabot, Danville & Barnet

- Joe's Pond & Molly's Pond in view of Camel's Hump and the Green Mountain Range, Cabot-Danville.
- Cabot's renown cheese factory & Visitor Center, Cabot.
- Picturesque Barnet Village, Connecticut River Valley.
- The beautiful hillside village of Peacham in autumn.
- Connecticut River in view of the CR Farm in Newbury.

Peacham & Newbury

Barnet, Peacham
Saint Johnsbury & Lyndon

- Autumn splendor, farmstead in Peacham.
- Farmstead with old Round Barn in Barnet.
- Fairbanks Museum, Main St., Saint Johnsbury.
- Maple Grove Maple Museum and Factory.
- Maple Grove Sugarhouse & Maple Museum.
- Picturesque Keiser Pond, Danville-Peacham.
- Miller's Run Bridge, built in 1878, Lyndon.
- Old Country Store, Saint Johnsbury.

Newport

- Newport, Gateway Ctr., Lake Memphremagog.
- Jay Peak as seen from Derby Lake, Derby.
- Saint Mary's Church, Newport.
- Lake Memphremagog & Owl's Head, Newport.
- Lake Willoughby & Mount Pisgah, Westmore.

Vermont's Beautiful Northeast Kingdom

Front Cover: Stowe / Mt. Mansfield

Other locations & page numbers:
1 Placid pond, Weston - Andover
24-25 Woodstock
46-47 East Corinth
66-67 Malletts Bay, Colchester
80 Mendon

Rear Cover: Cilley Bridge, Tunbridge

Clockwise: Quechee Gorge;
Trapp Family Lodge; Stowe
Gondola; Maria von Trapp with
daughter Maria; Sugarbush,
Warren; Rutland, view of Pico;
Wildflowers; Moose; Killington;
Northfield; Cow in Reading